DOLPHINS

BY RON HIRSCHI

BENCHMARK BOOKS

MARSHALL CAVENDISH
NEW YORK

Series Consultant
James Doherty
General Curator
Bronx Zoo, New York
Thanks to Paul Sieswerda, Curator, New York Aquarium, for his expert reading of this manuscript.

Benchmark Books
Marshall Cavendish
99 White Plains Road
Tarrytown, NY 10591–9001
www.marshallcavendish.u s

Library of Congress Cataloging-in-Publication Data
Hirschi, Ron.
Dolphins / by Ron Hirschi.
p. cm.–(Animals animals)
Includes bibliographical references and index.
Summary: Describes the physical characteristics, behavior, and habitat of this marine mammal.
ISBN 0-7614-1443-6
1. Dolphins–Juvenile literature. [1. Dolphins.] I. Title. II. Series.
QL737.C452 H57 2002
599.53–dc21
2001006992

Photo Research by Anne Burns Images
Cover Photo: Animals/Animals: Gerard Lacz
The photographs in this book are used by permission and through the courtesyof:
Animals/Animals: James Watt, 4, 19; Gerard Lacz, 17, 29; Peter Weiman, 20. *Visuals Unlimited*: Tom Walker, 6; A.J.Copley, 9; Marty Snyderman, 12;
Mike DeMocker, 23. *Peter Arnold*: Kelvin Aitken, 11, 27 (top); Mark Carwardine/Still Pictures, 26 (top), 40; Marilyn Kazmers, 27(middle), 32–33;
Michael Sewell 27 (lower); BIOS (M.Denis–Huot) 36; Jeffrey L. Rotman, 43. *Norbert Wu*: 26 (middle), 30, 31, 41; Peter Howorth/Mo Yung 14, 26
(lower). *Wolfgang Kaehler*: 24, 38. *Tom Stack & Associates*: Michael S. Nolan/Wildlife Images, 34.

Printed in China
3 5 6 4 2

CONTENTS

1
INTRODUCING DOLPHINS

The sea is calm, the day warm. Suddenly, the water explodes as two, ten, then twenty dolphins leap high into the air. They somersault, flip backward, and splash into the sea like Olympic divers. These are spinner dolphins and, unlike athletes competing for gold medals, they may leap just for fun.

Dolphins are well known for their playful behavior–one sign of intelligence in the animal kingdom. Other clues are their superior ability to communicate vocally and their large brain size.

You might think that dolphins are fish, but they are not. Dolphins are *mammals*. Unlike fish, they must come up to the surface for air. Mammals breathe through lungs rather than through gills. They are *warm–blooded* and give birth to live young that drink their mother's milk.

Dolphins are members of a group of mammals called

ONCE KILLED BY THE THOUSANDS IN TUNA NETS, SPINNER DOLPHINS CAN NOW LEAP MORE FREELY THANKS TO CHANGES IN FISHING METHODS.

THE WOLF OF THE SEA, THE ORCA, OR KILLER WHALE, IS THE LARGEST MEMBER OF THE FAMILY THAT INCLUDES DOLPHINS.

NOSE-TO-NOSE COMPARISON IS THE EASIEST WAY TO TELL A DOLPHIN FROM A PORPOISE.

PORPOISE   DOLPHIN

cetaceans–the whales. Whales are divided into two groups, those with teeth and those without. Most large whales lack teeth and strain their food from the water with brush–like *baleen*. Dolphins belong to the whale group with teeth. Other toothed whales include the much larger sperm whale and the killer, or orca, whale.

Scientists generally use the word dolphin to refer to any small–toothed whale with a beak or long nose.

The more than thirty *species*, or types, of dolphins swim

7

in all the world's oceans, but they are most abundant in warm, tropical seas. Dolphin *habitats* include the open ocean, coral reefs, sandy bays, fjords, and even the rims of mountains that poke up from the sea floor.

One of the most extraordinary things about dolphins in the wild is their relationship with others of their kind. Highly social, dolphins form *herds*, or groups, sometimes numbering as many as one million individuals. Smaller herds are more common. River dolphins usually live on their own, but can sometimes be found swimming in small groups of three or four.

Scientists believe the earliest whales appeared in the sea about 50 million years ago. At that time, there were shallow seas covering lands that are now much higher and drier. We have learned from *fossils* that whale ancestors spent some time on land. These early relatives of the

A LINK TO THE PAST—THE REMAINS OF A ONCE SMALLER ANCESTOR
OF THE WHALE.

whales reached lengths of about sixty feet (18 m). They fed
on fish and other sea life.

Not long ago, a scientist studying fossils in Egypt dis-
covered the remains of a prehistoric whale relative. This
forty-million-year-old fossil resembled today's whales
with one big difference–it had legs and feet.

There are still pieces missing that could link today's
streamlined dolphins more fully with those ancient
relatives. Scientists continue to search in likely locations,
studying the fascinating connection between past and present.

9

2
FACE-TO-FACE WITH DOLPHINS

Many dolphins are about the same size as people. The smallest include the Hector's dolphin at about five feet (1.3 m) and the Franciscana, or La Plata, dolphin, which may reach six feet (1.8 m) in length. The largest dolphins, such as the Risso's, or grampus, dolphin, reach up to twelve or thirteen feet (4 m).

Dolphin bodies may have spots or splashes of light and dark colors that form beautiful patterns. Bold black and white designs often color backs and bellies such as those on the Southern right whale dolphin. Dark backs help the dolphin blend into colorless, deep seas. Light bellies help them avoid hungry sharks looking up at them in sky-brightened surface waters.

The dolphin's torpedo-like shape allows it to move quickly through the water. A pair of flippers is used for

WHILE SWIMMING, DOLPHINS USUALLY BREATHE ONLY ONCE OR TWICE EACH MINUTE.

steering. Most dolphins have a *dorsal*, or top, fin. It lacks bones and, like a keel on the bottom of a boat, helps the dolphin swim a straight course. The fin and the dolphin's flippers can sense objects in the water. In this way, the dolphin avoids obstacles in its path.

12

SKILLED SWIMMERS,
DOLPHINS ARE ABLE TO
GLIDE THROUGH BRIGHT
SUNLIT WATERS AS WELL
AS THE DARKEST AND
STORMIEST SEAS.

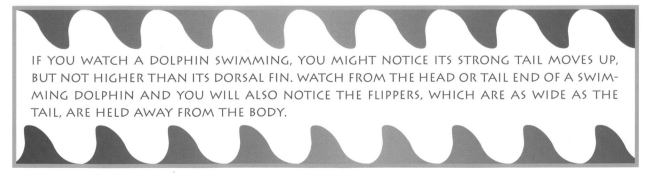

IF YOU WATCH A DOLPHIN SWIMMING, YOU MIGHT NOTICE ITS STRONG TAIL MOVES UP,
BUT NOT HIGHER THAN ITS DORSAL FIN. WATCH FROM THE HEAD OR TAIL END OF A SWIM-
MING DOLPHIN AND YOU WILL ALSO NOTICE THE FLIPPERS, WHICH ARE AS WIDE AS THE
TAIL, ARE HELD AWAY FROM THE BODY.

MALE RISSO'S DOLPHINS ARE OFTEN SCARRED WITH TOOTH MARKS FROM THEIR FIGHTS WITH OTHER MALES. THEY LACK THE LONG SNOUTS MOST OF THEIR RELATIVES SPORT, AND THEIR FOREHEADS HAVE A DISTINCT MELON-SHAPED BULGE.

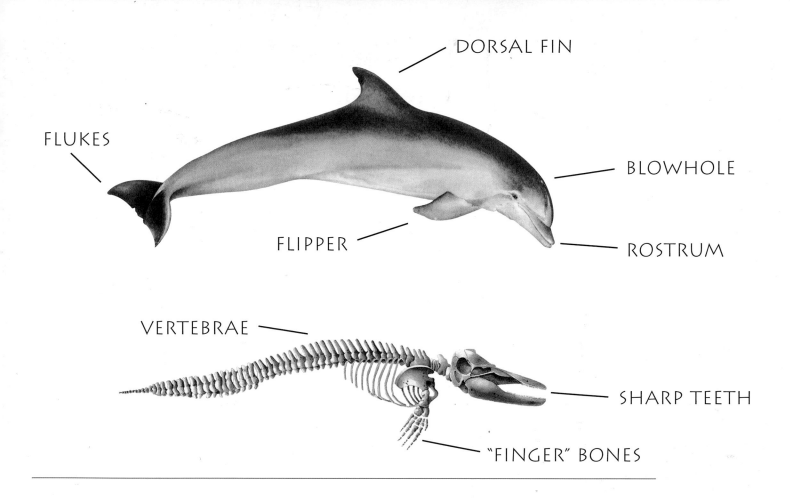

DORSAL FIN

FLUKES

BLOWHOLE

FLIPPER

ROSTRUM

VERTEBRAE

SHARP TEETH

"FINGER" BONES

The dolphin's tail is horizontal. It is made up of two sections, or lobes, called *flukes*. Strong muscles along the sides of the dolphin body move the tail up and down, propelling it through the water.

Dolphin skin is smooth, not studded with the many scales that cover a fish body. Underneath the skin is a thick layer of fat called blubber, which helps to keep the animal warm.

Dolphins do not breathe through their mouth. Instead, they have an opening, known as the blowhole, on top of their head. This is essentially a nostril, which, like your nose, is used to breathe in fresh air. Dolphins swim to the surface to spout water out and then take air in through this opening. Muscles attached to the skull close the blowhole when the dolphin dives back underwater.

The skeleton shows a close relationship with other mammals, including humans. Within the paddle-shaped flippers, for instance, there are five "finger" bones.

Dolphins can feel objects by touching with flippers and other body parts. In fact, dolphins seem to enjoy the sense of touch a great deal, often moving close to others in body-to-body or flipper-to-body contact not unlike humans holding hands.

Dolphins use their sense of taste differently than humans do. Special sensors on the adult dolphin's tongue taste chemicals that tell them a potential mate is near. Baby dolphins appear to be able to taste their mother's milk.

Tiny ear openings just behind the eyes are probably not used for hearing. Some scientists believe that dolphins receive sound through their lower jaw. The sound travels along a nerve to the middle ear, inner ear, and finally, to the hearing centers in the brain.

JUST LIKE YOU AND YOUR FRIENDS, DOLPHINS RECOGNIZE EACH OTHER BY THEIR VOICES.

A dolphin's eyes are located on either side of its head. They function independently, allowing the dolphin to see all around itself, including straight ahead.

Scents drifting through the air are of little use to the sea–dwelling dolphin. But sounds filling the ocean are critical to its survival. Dolphins make many sounds and use their well–developed voice and sense of hearing to communicate with others, catch food, and find their way through the sea.

Dolphins click. Dolphins whistle. They make sounds that our ears cannot hear. Some of these noises bounce off of fish and other objects. Depending on how quickly or slowly the echo returns, the dolphin can tell how close it is to the *prey*. This method of finding prey is called *echolocation.*

Dolphins in the same group can communicate with each other vocally. They make a series of sounds to send messages like "help!" or "stick together!" When they hear another dolphin in distress they will go to its aid or rally together to keep predators away. Individual dolphins each have their own distinctive sound, by which others in the group can identify them.

THE AVERAGE DOLPHIN SWIMS AT A RATE OF BETWEEN THREE AND SEVEN MILES (5–11 KM) PER HOUR. THEIR MAXIMUM SPEED CAN REACH UP TO TWENTY-TWO MILES (35 KM) PER HOUR. OCEANIC DOLPHINS DIVE TO DEPTHS OF 10 TO 150 FEET (3 TO 45 M) TO CATCH FOOD. THE DEEPEST DIVE ON RECORD IS 1,500 FEET (457 M) BY A BOTTLENOSE DOLPHIN. IT IS POSSIBLE FOR A DIVE TO LAST UP TO FIFTEEN MINUTES.

3
DOLPHINS OF THE WORLD

The dolphins that are most familiar to us are the oceanic dolphins. There are over thirty species of these ocean dwellers. The most common species seen in marine parks and zoos is the bottlenose dolphin. Some bottlenoses spend much of their time in shallow water where we can see them from the seashore. They have a long *rostrum*, or snout. Their backs are grayish with a pointed dorsal fin and their bellies may be white or pink. Bottlenose dolphins usually grow to about eight feet (2.4 m) and weigh about two hundred pounds (91 kg). Recent studies have shown that bottlenose dolphins may prefer to live in areas with a variety of habitats. Coral reefs, mangrove shores, and sea–grass beds serve as feeding grounds, while nearby deep waters are needed for escape.

THE BOTTLENOSE DOLPHIN LIVES CLOSE TO SHORE ON THE ATLANTIC AND GULF COASTS.

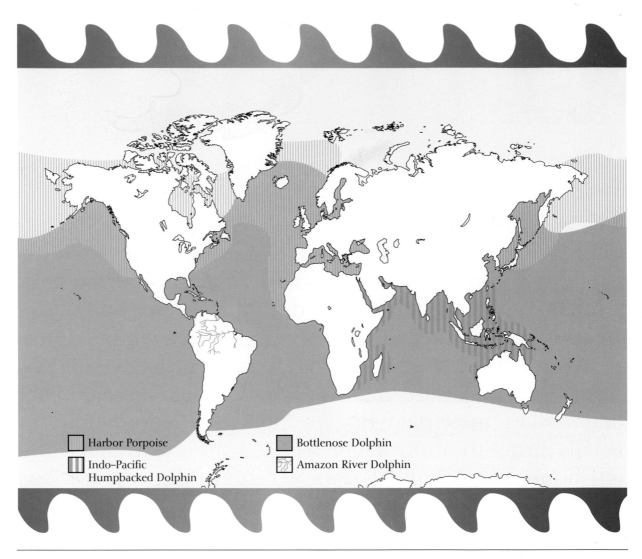

SHOWN HERE ARE NORMAL RANGES FOR FOUR SPECIES OF DOLPHIN

Spinner dolphins are true acrobats. They can leap into the air, spinning as many as four times before diving back into the sea. Spinners can also leap up and flip, tail over head, before landing back in the water with a great splash.

Spinners are slender with a long snout that slopes gently from their forehead. Color patterns vary around the world as do the shapes of the tall dorsal fins. Some spinner dorsal fins are near perfect triangles, while others may slope forward or curve back.

The small and stout dusky dolphin swims southern oceans, including the waters of South America and New Zealand. Reaching six feet (1.8 m) in length, they have distinctive color patterns. The tip of their short snout is dark. Two streaks of white and gray seem painted onto their otherwise dark sides.

Right whale dolphins, among the most elegantly shaped sea creatures, lack a dorsal fin. Their streamlined body shoots through the waves as they leap into the air with little effort. Southern right whale dolphins are colored

DUSKY DOLPHINS LEAPING ALONG THE COAST OF NEW ZEALAND. SCIENTISTS BELIEVE THEY MAY LEAP TO ATTRACT EACH OTHER.

like a penguin. The black of its back hides this dolphin's eye while the white color of its belly curves above the flipper and over the short snout.

The Northern right whale dolphin is somewhat darker and larger than the Southern. Living mainly in the open ocean it grows to about ten feet (3 m). Its scientific name translates as "smooth dolphin of the northern wind." Known to swim in large groups, little information is available about its life history.

24

The baiji, or Chinese river dolphin, is one of the rarest mammals on Earth. These animals have a longer, more narrow rostrum than the bottlenose. Needle-sharp teeth help the baiji catch fish in its Yangtze River home, the only place where these dolphins live. Baiji are related to ocean-dwelling dolphins. Their ancestors were isolated in Chinese rivers, and over twenty million years they adapted to freshwater. Scientists recently reported results of a ten-year study that estimate one hundred or fewer baiji remaining in the Yangtze River. Other species of river dolphin swim the Amazon, La Plata, Orinoco, Irriwaddy, Indus, and Ganges Rivers.

The Ganges River dolphin has tiny, poorly developed eyes. Lacking a lens, the eye lets in light but cannot focus images, so the dolphin is nearly blind. To find food, the Ganges dolphin often swims on its side feeling for prey in the bottom ooze with large, paddle-shaped flippers. Then they snatch fish, turtles, and other food with their long snout. People also call this dolphin Susu in imitation of the sound it makes when it comes to the surface to breathe. The Susu or Ganges River dolphin is pale brown with a slight hump in place of a dorsal fin. They may grow to about eight feet (2.4 m) in length.

DOLPHIN SPECIES

Fraser's dolphin
7.5 feet (2.26 m)
408 pounds (185 kg)

Amazon River dolphin
9.8 feet (3 m)
269 pounds (122 kg)

Risso's dolphin
12 feet (4 m)
800 pounds (363 kg)

Atlantic spotted dolphin
8 feet (2.4 m)
265 pounds (120 kg)

Pacific white–sided dolphin
7 feet (2.13 m) up to
300 pounds (131 kg)

Right whale dolphin
10 feet (3.28 m)
180 pounds (81 kg)

4
DOLPHIN LIFESTYLES

Most dolphins eat only fish, but their diet also includes squid, crab, shrimp, and other small sea life. They are able to swim faster than most of their prey, chasing them down and gripping them with sharp teeth. One such prey, the flying fish, makes catching supper a real challenge. The dolphin must twist and leap as the fish skips across the waves trying to escape the dolphin's grasp.

Bottlenose dolphins swallow their prey whole and sometimes feed in an unusual way. Researchers have observed a lone bottlenose dolphin blowing bursts of bubbles beneath schools of fish. The bubbles pushed the school into a tight ball near the surface where the dolphin could more easily catch its prey.

DOLPHINS ARE OFTEN COMPARED TO PEOPLE, IN PART BECAUSE OF THEIR TIGHTLY KNIT SOCIAL GROUPS.

Most dolphin dinners are captured near the surface, but dolphins have been known to dive to depths as great as 1,500 feet (457 m). Some of their prey live in the deep, dark reaches of the sea. These include animals equipped with their own lights. Among these dolphin delicacies is the lantern fish.

Lantern fish are *bioluminescent*, producing light in *photo–phores*, which are tiny spots on their bodies powered by chemical reactions. Some lantern fish have the light spots between their eyes. Known as headlight fish, they

glow in night seas like miniature fast food restaurants, attracting hungry dolphin diners.

Some dolphins specialize in shallow water feeding, often nosing along the bottom in search of a meal. Here, they catch fish or crabs. But bottom feeding can be a risky business. Stingrays live on the sea floor, using their sharp spines as a defense against predators. Dolphins are some—times seen with the spines stuck in their snouts like thorns. Others have not been so lucky. Both bottlenose dolphins and killer whales sometimes swallow stingrays. Members of both species have been found dead with stingray spines puncturing their internal organs.

A MOTHER AND CALF
SPOTTED DOLPHIN SWIM
IN HARMONY NEAR
THE BAHAMA ISLANDS.

FIVE SPINNER DOLPHINS SWIM IN A LINE. FISHING TOGETHER OFTEN MEANS GREATER SUCCESS.

The Franciscana, or La Plata, dolphin of South America lives in an *estuary*, the place where rivers meet the sea. Like a heron or diving seabird, the Franciscana uses its excellent vision and long snout to snatch small fish, squid, and crabs from the rich shallows.

Feeding is sometimes a social activity for dolphins. They may spread out like the front line of a football team, cooperating to catch fish. Individuals may swim away from the group to catch a meal, only to return later to rub against others like friendly Labrador retrievers. Dolphins touch one another often, swimming close and playfully.

Females typically swim together, and as with dolphin groups in general, they may pay a high price for abandoning the group. Lone females with babies might lose young ones without the protection given by other group members.

Baby dolphins, called *calves*, develop inside their mother's body for about twelve months. Several months before she gives birth, the mother chooses another female dolphin to help her. This helper, commonly known as an "auntie," travels with the mother and looks after her until the baby is born. Calves are born tail first and are carried to the surface by the mother for their first breath.

Once it has inhaled the life-giving breath of air, a new-born dolphin nudges its mother, searching for nipples tucked within two slits on her belly. The baby's tongue extends to the tip of its snout. The mother's milk is far richer in fat than that of any land mammal. This nourishing liquid diet helps the dolphin grow quickly. Even though it may swallow freshly caught fish within six months, the young dolphin often continues to nurse for as long as two years. Newborn dusky dolphins are a tiny twenty-four

SPOTTED DOLPNINS OFTEN TRAVEL IN LARGE GROUPS.

inches (60 cm) in length while the bottlenose measures about three-and-a-half feet (107 cm) at birth.

Young dolphins will rest atop and alongside their mothers, often hitching a ride. Water streaming past the fast-swimming mother swirls in a way that can wrap around and hold the calf on. Some mother dolphins will even carry a baby that has died in infancy.

Young bottlenose dolphins stay with their mothers for many years. The mother will give birth again, but usually not for three to seven years. Both males and females are considered juveniles–the phase of life spent before they become adults–for about ten years. During this time they learn to find food and develop other skills critical for survival and for raising their own young.

Research suggests that dolphins often live to be about twenty years old, though some scientists say striped dolphins can live to be fifty. Many threats, both natural and unnatural, shorten this lifespan. Tiger sharks, great white sharks, and killer whales all attack and kill dolphins, especially the young. But the greatest threat to dolphins and other marine life is the human one.

5

DOLPHINS AND PEOPLE

People love dolphins. The playful antics of bottlenose dolphins have long been a favorite attraction at zoos and marine parks. Dolphins actually seem to enjoy the company of humans, and children in particular. In spite of this, humans have also hunted dolphins for centuries.

In the distant past dolphins were hunted with hand thrown spears. In more modern times, nets captured large numbers of dolphins unintentionally. This was especially true of tuna fisheries. Tuna often swim with dolphins. Nets were set around herds of dolphins, and thousands were killed. Many people were outraged by this and protested the needless killing. New fishing methods were designed to avoid dolphin capture, and the trapping of dolphins in tuna nets was greatly reduced.

THOUGH PROTECTED BY THE MARINE MAMMAL ACT, DOLPHINS LIKE THIS PAIR ARE KEPT FOR RESEARCH. THEY ARE ALSO A POPULAR DRAW AT MARINE PARKS.

FRASER'S DOLPHINS

THERE ARE MANY DOLPHINS THAT SCIENTISTS KNOW VERY LITTLE ABOUT. MAYBE YOU WILL BE THE ONE TO MAKE DISCOVERIES ABOUT THE FOLLOWING TYPES:

FRASER'S DOLPHIN: THEY LIVE IN LARGE HERDS. ALMOST NOTHING IS KNOWN ABOUT THEIR FOOD, SOCIAL LIFE, AND COMMUNICATION.

ROUGH-TOOTHED DOLPHIN: MUCH HAS BEEN LEARNED ABOUT THESE DOLPHINS IN CAPTIVITY, BUT LITTLE IS KNOWN ABOUT THEIR LIFE IN THE WILD.

HUMPBACKED DOLPHIN: THEY SURVIVE IN POLLUTED SEAS NEAR HONG KONG, BUT CAN THEY ENDURE AS OCEAN HABITAT CONDITIONS WORSEN? WHAT CAN WE DO TO CLEAN UP THEIR OCEAN HOME?

HOURGLASS DOLPHIN: THESE SMALL DOLPHINS LIVE ONLY IN ANTARCTIC WATERS WHERE THEY ARE THOUGHT TO BE SAFE FROM HUMAN ACTIVITIES. WILL THEY REMAIN SAFE AS GREATER PRESSURE IS PLACED ON EXPLOITATION OF SOUTHERN SEAS?

SCIENTISTS, FISHERMEN, AND CONCERNED CITIZENS HAVE HELPED SAVE DOLPHINS FROM CAPTURE IN NETS. SADLY, BLUEFIN TUNA LIKE THESE ARE NOW THOUGHT TO BE IN GREATER DANGER THAN THE DOLPHINS.

You can learn how to help dolphins by contacting the Defenders of Wildlife, The Whale and Dolphin Conservation Society, and the International Rivers Network. This last organization works in China looking for ways to save the baiji from becoming *extinct*.

Many dolphins and dolphin relatives are still in danger. More Dall porpoises are killed each year than any other whale, large or small, with as many as 30,000 killed each year by Japanese fishermen.

Japanese and Taiwanese hunters also kill spotted and striped dolphins for food. In the Solomon Islands, people are known to kill dolphins to obtain teeth used for necklaces.

The greatest threats to river dolphins occur where dams alter the freshwater habitats of rare species and their prey.

In 200 B.C., Chinese naturalists wrote "The river is teeming with baiji, a white dolphin which has a large belly and a long beak with sharp teeth." Some Chinese considered this river dolphin a goddess swimming in the Yangtze, but changes to its environment now threaten the baiji's survival.

Existing dams already block the path of the baiji, preventing them from swimming into *tributary* streams where they once fed or reared their calves. More destructive dams are now planned, including the largest hydroelectric project on Earth, the Three Gorges dam.

This massive dam will flood the homes of more than one million people. As waters rise behind the concrete river barrier, nature preserves once meant to protect the few remaining baiji will be lost for all time.

In the 1980s, when threats to the baiji came mostly from boat traffic on the river, Chinese authorities tried to save the dolphins. If the Three Gorges dam floods this natural river habitat, the baiji will not be able to swim to a new home. Scientists fear it will be the first dolphin to become extinct due to humans.

Even though some dolphins are in danger, people have worked hard to save others. Both spinner and spotted dolphins were saved from needless deaths when people changed tuna fishing methods. As we become more aware of the problems facing the dolphin and its ocean habitat, we can find new ways to prevent further damage.

THE OCEAN IS HOME TO MANY INTELLIGENT CREATURES. THE SURVIVAL OF OCTOPUS, DOLPHINS, AND EVEN HUMANS DEPENDS ON OUR CONTINUAL RESEARCH AND PROTECTION OF THE VAST REACHES OF THE SEA.

baleen: interlocking plates hanging from the upper jaw that whales use to strain food

bioluminescent: an animal that is able to give off light as a result of a chemical process

calves: baby dolphins

cetacean: the group of mammals that includes all whales, including dolphins and porpoises

dorsal: back, as in the fin on the back of a dolphin or fish

echolocation: the ability to find an object using sound emission and reception

estuary: the place where salt and fresh waters meet

extinct: a plant or animal that has vanished for all time

fluke: one of the lobes of a dolphin's tail

fossil: hardened remains or traces of an animal or plant that lived long ago

habitat: type of environment in which an animal lives

herd: a group of dolphins

mammals: warm–blooded animals that have body hair and give birth to live young that nurse on their mother's milk

photophores: tiny dots on some sea creatures that emit light from chemical reactions inside their bodies

prey: animals that become the food of others

rostrum: beak, or upper snout, of a dolphin

species: a group of animals with similar features that are able to reproduce

tributary: a stream that flows into another body of water

warm–blooded: having the ability to burn food to create body heat

45

FIND OUT MORE

WEBSITES

Defenders of Wildlife
www.kidsplanet.org

International Rivers Network
www.irn.org

The Whale and Dolphin Conservation Society
www.wdcs.org

The Whale Center of New England
www.whalecenter.org

BOOKS AND VIDEOS

Berg, Cami. *D is for Dolphin*. Santa Fe, NM: Windom
    Books, 1991.
Fowler, Allan. *Friendly Dolphins*. Danbury, CT: Children's
    Press, 1997.
Morris, Robert. *Dolphin*. New York: HarperCollins, 1975.
Robinson, Claire. *Dolphins*. Crystal Lake, IL: Heinemann
    Library, 1999.

The Blue Planet. Seas of Life. Narrated by Sir David Attenborough. Discovery Chanel, 2002.

Additional information can be found by visiting major aquariums and their websites, including the Monterey Bay Aquarium.

ABOUT THE AUTHOR

Ron Hirschi grew up at the edge of the sea in the Pacific Northwest. A growing compassion for all life soon turned him to the study of seals and other sea life. Ron now divides his time between work as a biologist, writing, and work–ing with young people on ecology projects that include the restoration of his native shores. Ron is the author of many other books including WHALEMAIL, a fun–filled account of the migration of humpbacked whales from Alaska to Hawaii.

INDEX

Page numbers for illustrations are in **boldface.**